CW01080557

Abit's Secret

Overstanding the Warrior's Province.

Let's explore our personal space with this life-long-learning story while it introduces key science & maths ideas for us along the way.

This is an imaginary pop-up book that journeys deeply into space to reveal its beautiful creative patterns (as found when studying life with maths and science). As an 'edutaining' story expressed in the classic የጥምር:ዕውቀት:: unifiedknowledge way, it connects us to the deepest ideas of energy, matter and mind as children, families and the young at heart globally. Parents and teachers work through this story with the young Ones until they can fly through it themselves as truly independent learners. Remember, as interests pop-up nurture and guide them.

Three, young, African Crowned.Crane birds catch a glimpse of Abit's inner world. The wise Praying Mantis 'Abit' allows them a taste of her wonderful insights, Abit's Secret.

Author:
Astehmari Batekun

Publisher:
Peoplescience Intelligence Unit

PEOPLESCIENCE
INTELLIGENCE UNIT

Abit's Secret - Overstanding the Warrior's Province
by Astehmari Batekun

Books may be purchased by contacting the publisher and author at:

Publisher:
Peoplescience Intelligence Unit
c/o Abundance Centres (UK), 86 Vestry Road, London SE5 8PQ

Web: www.peoplescience.org.uk
Tel: +44 20 8144 1720

Peoplescience Intelligence Unit and Astehmari Batekun are trading functions of Ras Astehmari Batekun (Khu) Un Ltd

Author: Astehmari Batekun
Story Style: Ephat Mujuru, (Zimbabwean Mbira master)
Illustrator: Lee A White
Editor: Mama D, (Community Centred Knowledge)
Pedagogy: Unifiedknowledge (የጥምር፡ዕውቀት፡፡ Yeht'mr Urwuk'eht)
                     c/o Schools Of Unified Learning (SOUL)

ISBN: 978-0-9528229-8-1

First Edition, Community Builder Series.

Printed in Germany

Content

The Story:

The Pedagogy

The Appendix

እግዚር ይምስጋን፦ ሐሺማ ተዋጊ አሳብ፦

Beginning

A long time ago. A long, long time ago.

In the old dark lands of Kush, in Africa, deep, deep, deep in the countryside there lived a wise insect called Abit.

Abit, the praying mantid, was a great friend of the Winchi family, a mighty flock of Crowned Cranes.

They used to sing together.

Now I want you to sing this song:

 የም ኺ ጤና ይስጥልኝ:: ኺ የም ጤና ይስጥልኝ::
om i t'ena yist'lng. i om t'ena yist'lng.

የም ኺ ጤና ይስጥልኝ:: ኺ የም ጤና ይስጥልኝ::
om i t'ena yist'lng. i om t'ena yist'lng.

They used to dance with her.

They were both very good dancers.

Abit would dance like this…

and Winchi would dance like this…

The young Winchi birds used to enjoy
Abit's dancing because she was
a great warrior.

09

Pleeease!

One day after playing with the young Ones Abit fell asleep. When she woke up she realized that she had shed all of her skin and was now much greater in body and mind.

Although she had shed her skin she was still inside the old shell, so she climbed out and began carefully cleaning herself from the tips of her feet, to the crown of her head.

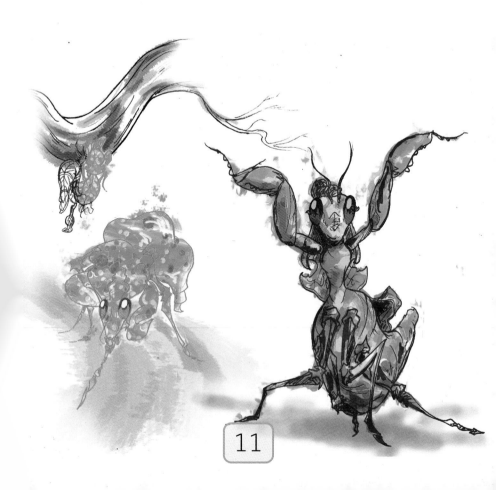

11

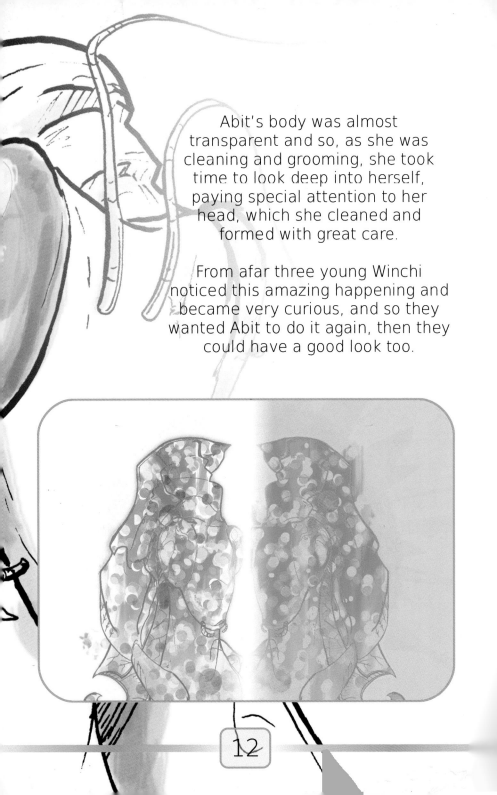

Abit's body was almost
transparent and so, as she was
cleaning and grooming, she took
time to look deep into herself,
paying special attention to her
head, which she cleaned and
formed with great care.

From afar three young Winchi
noticed this amazing happening and
became very curious, and so they
wanted Abit to do it again, then they
could have a good look too.

The young birds went up to Abit and said "Abit! Abit!

Please do that again? You know, shed your skin so that we can look inside and see.

Your skin we want you to shed, reveal to us your bodies and your head".

Quite surprised, Abit said "I can't just drop my skin
like a hat! This is my adult skin and I like it.
Now that's that ! ".

As she spoke her skin began to harden and take on its
natural brown colour, just like the surrounding leaves.

14

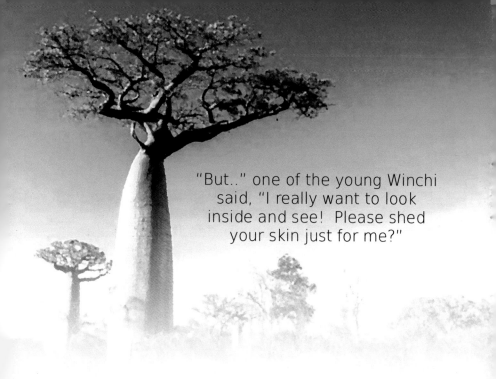

"But.." one of the young Winchi said, "I really want to look inside and see! Please shed your skin just for me?"

"My skin I'll never shed and I'm sure I'll regret it if you get into my head!", said Abit.

You see Abit knew that when ever she shed her skin she was completely revealed, and she was especially shy about revealing her head.

Even when she went to bed she protected her head. Even when she was cleaning herself she'd always spend more time cleaning her head, making sure that it was balanced and bright.

Abit loved her head because it was full of the purest light.

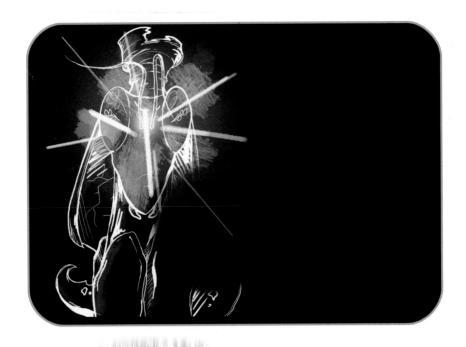

Another young One came up to Abit and said,
"I'll be your best friend! Please, please shed your
skin again?".

"My skin I'll never shed and i'm sure I'll regret it if you
get into my head. Don't let me tell you again,
You nuh hear what the I has said!"

"Please, please, pleeease!!"
the youngest Winchi begged.

17

Going in

Eventually, after some time, the young Ones
persuaded Abit, who was touched by their
great interest.

Proudly Abit said, "I'm a mature adult now, so my
skin I'll never shed, but just this once you may view
my head. My head is a serious site, highly blessed
and not just for fun, what you see inside you can't
explain to anyone. When you're older, and know
things well, then and only then will you
be able to tell."

So Abit flew up
high, right in front of
the sun.

The light was so bright
that now the young
Ones could see right
through Abit's body.

In One voice the three
young birds said, "OK!
We'll not tell anyone.
We'll NEVER tell."

19

They looked carefully and were surprised to see that Abit had a beautiful well inside her head.

Yes! A well... a deep, deep, deep hole with fresh warm spring water at the bottom of it. Abit also had a rather large fire radiating from within her abdomen, but this didn't seem so important compared to the well, which greatly attracted the young Ones' attention.

As they looked deep into Abit's head, their collective mind filled with thoughts of the future.

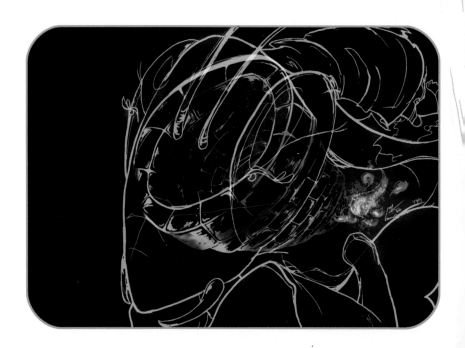

The young birds took one of their small thoughts and dropped it into the well.

After a time there was a faint splash, which made them even more curious.

Using their imagination they began to fly, in a spiral form, down into the well.

Abit always enjoyed it when young Ones used their imagination, so she let them explore the well.

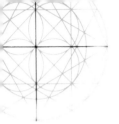

Entrance

After a time the three
had reached the bottom of the well.

The water was warm and sweet scented.

They were simply amazed that
such a thing could exist.

Before even hearing the question Abit's voice
spoke to them.

"This is the entrance to my province. እኔ የተዋጊ ግዛት
(ur.ne : yeh.teh.wa.gi : g.za.t::), I-Warrior-Province.
It is my space, I am responsible for everything in this
place and so I keep it peaceful at all times. I know it
very well, if you listen, its secrets I will tell. Knowing
my place allows me to know all space, in every place.
This knowledge brings me peace and freedom from
haste. The knowledge is great, you have to be very
brave to enter here, truly there's no room for fear.
So... if you want to leave now, just fly back out.
I'll say no more, I'll never tell."

The three Winchi's curiosity
was just too great.

With excitement in their voices they asked Abit
how to enter the **ግዛት** g.za.t ::

ግዛት::

." እግዝር ይምስጋን:: ሐሺማ ተዋጊ አሳብ::

(ur.g.z.r : yi.m.s.ga.n :: ha.shi.ma : teh.wa.gi : a.sa.b ::)

Creator be praised, Respect the Warrior Idea

Look into the water young Ones, study the patterns,
the waves... and be in harmony with them...
feel how they behave."

This didn't make complete sense to the young birds,
however, as they looked deeply into the water they
gradually began to feel it all about themselves.

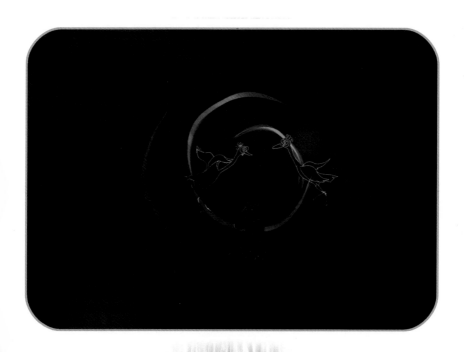

In an instant
the three where submerge in
a whole new innerworld.

The water was strange,
they could breath naturally in it,
and they could move freely in it too.
It was warm, light and seemed to
penetrate their whole body.

The entrance was no longer visible,
the young birds now moved as
a perfectly unified trinity, surrounded
by this strange substance for as far as
the eye (i) could see.

It felt like being in an
infinite amount of... jelly.

The Five

Moments passed and then, in the distance, the young Ones saw a small light, so, as one body they moved towards it. As they got closer they realized that the light had a triangular form.

But as they got closer still,
they realized it was a cube.

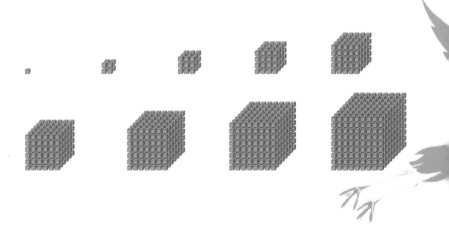

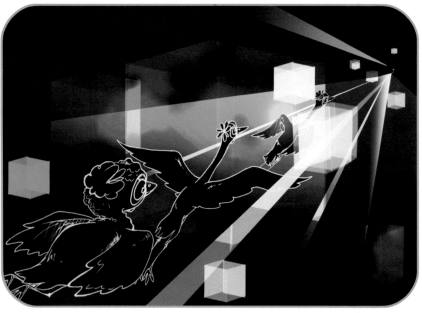

As they continued to advance they could now see one side of the shape, which appeared as a square.

On closer inspection they saw
a circle inside the square.

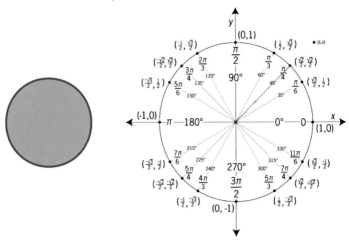

Now they were right up close and she could see that the circle was actually a sphere and standing inside the sphere... was... Abit.

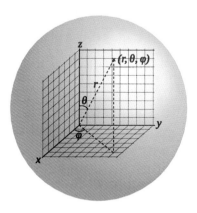

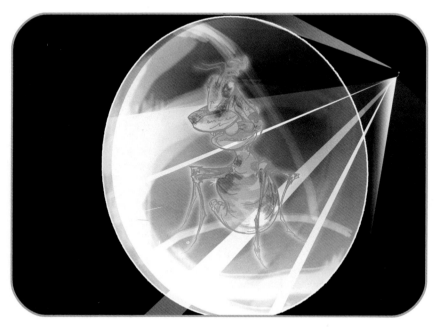

Abit began to speak.

"When the I entered this space it was empty, a.l.bo ::
There were no boundaries and no others.

This is the mindspace and from here One can create
all things, the landspace. Now... the distance
between the things One creates is the airspace.
Mindspace, landspace and airspace are the three
types of space that make up the g.za.t ::

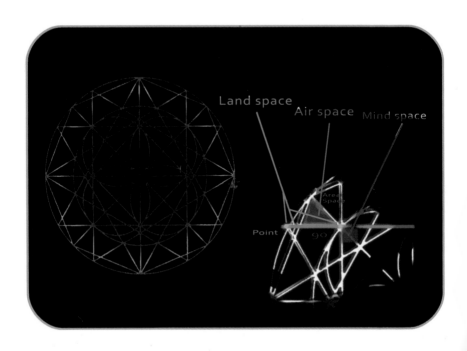

Essentially they are One and exist in perfect **ኣንድነት** (ah.n.d.neh.t), which means they are in "unity" with each other.

The three are held together by this watery jellylike substance, which is really the purest form of life-field there is.

In the gzat we call it darklight or **ብርሃን : ጨለማ ::** (b.r.ha.n : ch'eh.leh.ma ::) "light without light".

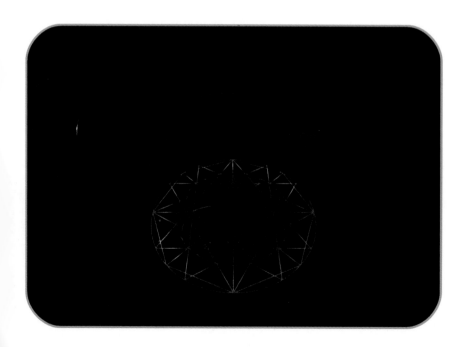

It surrounds you, it's within you, you come from it, it comes from you and it's an essence of everything in existence. Even natural light is made from b.r.ha.n : ch'eh.leh.ma ::

"Wow…" the young birds said, but Abit had not finished. "Now when the I (you) saw the light and began travelling towards it one became two (I and I) and the three types of space were realized… ya get me?"

Triangle: A two-dimensional shape with three sides and three angles, whose sum is always 180° (in Euclidean Geometry). Three-sided polygon. The first nine triangle numbers; 1 3 6 10 15 21 28 36 45. The Dankira (dance) movement that relates to this shape is the Ngoma Triangle.

Cube: A three-dimensional form with six square sides (faces) of equal area, in which the angle between any two adjacent sides is at a right angle. A regular hexahedron. The first nine cube numbers; 1 8 27 64 125 216 343 512 729. The Dankira (dance) movement that relates to the cube is Dankira Huleht applied 4 times with a 90° counter-clockwise rotation. Dankira Huleht Cubed.

Square: A two-dimensional shape with four sides of equal length and four right angles (90°) A four-sided regular polygon. The first nine square numbers; 1 4 9 16 25 36 49 64 81. The Dankira (dance) movement that relates to this shape is the Ngoma Triangle, a leg change and then another Ngoma. Triangle. The feet are placed at the four corners of the square. Precise right angles must be observed to move on the Ngoma Square.

Circle: A perfectly round, closed and single lined two-dimensional shape, which maintains a constant distance (radius) from its centre. Its perimetre is called a circumference. The numbers that relate to circles; 1, 360, π and its worth thinking about the radian ratio too. The Dankira (dance) movement that relates to this shape is the rotational aspect of Winchi Ngoma.

Sphere: A three-dimensional form with one encapsulating surface, ever point of which is equidistant from its centre. A globe or ball. The numbers that relate to this shape are; mysterious. The Dankira (dance) movements that relate to the sphere are rotation about an axis, rotation about a point external to its centre (orbit), 'wobble' (as a spinning top does) and/or rolling. With simply one surface, a sphere faces all directions; looking inward to and outward from the centre point.

Hmmm!" The young Ones groomed their heads.
"As you can see there are five important shapes in the
g.za.t :: the triangle, the cube, the square, the circle and
the sphere. When I took responsibility for my g.za.t I
began to realize that everything in it expressed
patterns, most of which are related to the
five important shapes and forms.

I began to study and reapply these patterns, which is
why I'm naturally a mathematician, a teh.wa.gi and a
dancer. Each one of these shapes has numbers that are
related to them and they have movement that relates
to them too... let me show you what I mean."

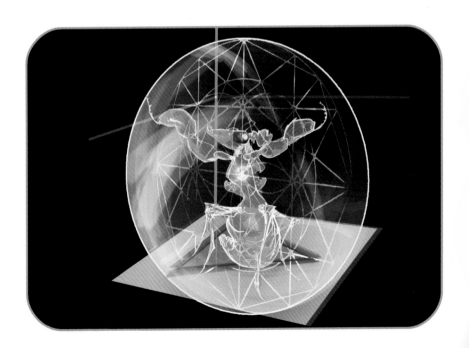

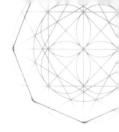

Mind Matter

"Now young Ones… listen carefully.

I share these things with you because you have shown interest in understanding ur.ne : yeh.teh.wa.gi : g.za.t :: I-Warrior-Province. In all ways, when you have gained interest you can accomplish great learning. ha.shi.ma."

The child smiled.

"As I have said, the g.za.t is made from three types of space; land, air and mind. All of these are made from one substance, darklight, also known as ብርሃን:ጨለማ:: b.r.ha.n : ch'eh.leh.ma :: the 'light without light'.

Here, in the g.za.t, you can feel it all about and within you, but on earth it's not so easy to detect. In fact, even the mind can be hard to observe, but let me tell you another great secret... The way to know One's mindspace is by the things that come through it and by peacefully observing its principles.

This is why, my children, we must study the patterns and forms of landspace (which are things) and airspace (which is the perceived space between things).

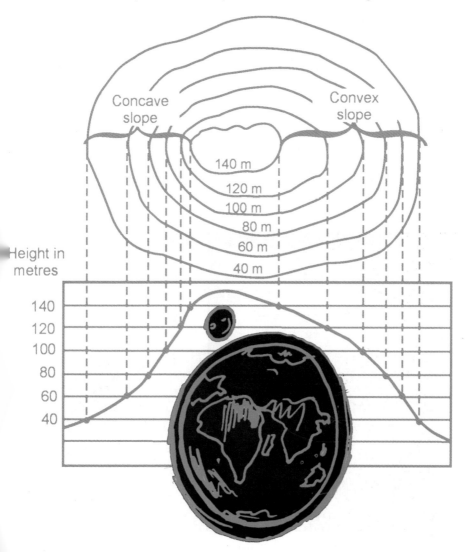

There are some other important things you need to know about **ብርሃን:ጨለማ::** b.r.ha.n : ch'eh.leh.ma :: this most essential substance in the universe.

Firstly, it has two qualities, which can be likened, to fire and water or as positive and negative qualities, they compliment each other in an endless struggle to maintain balance.

Secondly, this b.r.ha.n : ch'eh.leh.ma :: vibrates, and because everything in the universe is moving the vibrations form wave patterns.

All of this movement causes a powerful and vast matrix (network) of bonding forces between all things.

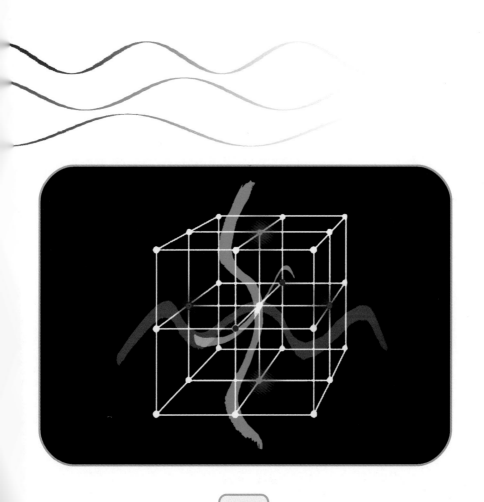

Now on earth, landspace and airspace are
known as matter and matter typically exists in three
forms; solids, liquids and gases. All of which are made
from atoms, which are made from electrons (negative
qualities), neutrons (neutral qualities), protons
(positive qualities) and other smaller things,
and all of these atomic elements are made
from b.r.ha.n : ch'eh.leh.ma ::

I hope you're still listening young Ones!

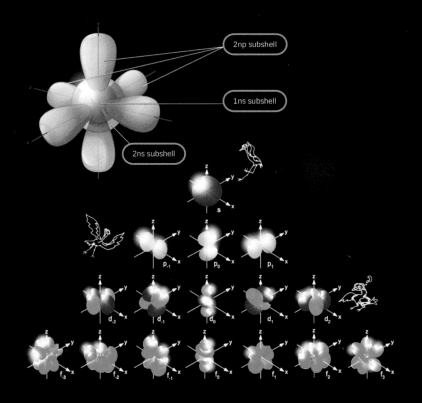

The form matter takes is related to the density (compactness or togetherness) of the atomic elements that make it.

A very dense arrangement, one that has the greatest bonding forces between the atoms, manifests as a solid, which has a fixed shape, and fixed volume.

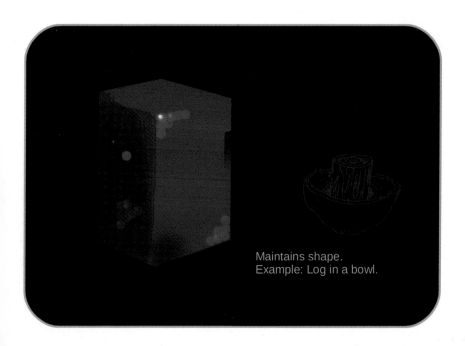

Maintains shape.
Example: Log in a bowl.

In liquids, the bonding forces are not as great, thus, liquids do not have a fixed shape, but they do have a fixed volume.

This can be seen by the fact that when you pour a liquid into different shaped containers it will take on the shape of the container, without changing its three dimensional capacity, which is its volume or amount.

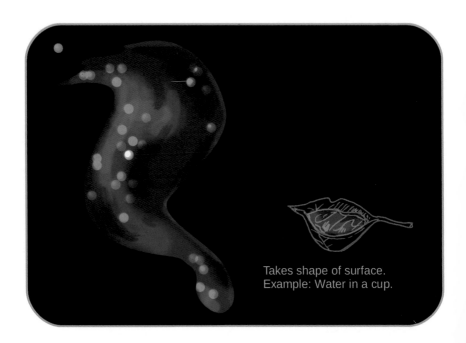

Takes shape of surface.
Example: Water in a cup.

In a gas the bonding force is so slight that the elements and molecules are perceived as independent to each other.

It has no fixed shaped or fixed volume.

The shape and volume of gases are defined by its container or surrounding forces.

Fills containing area.
Example: Air in balloon

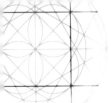

That rocks

Without warning Abit's sphere exploded and its gaseous contents spread throughout the space until it was invisible.

Abit had disappeared also.

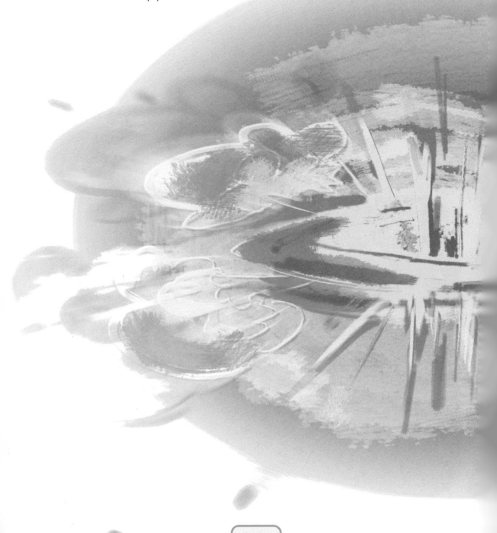

From the ether Abit's voice spoke to the Winchi trinity. "Do this mental activity, and then answer my question. Imagine a huge bolder, and a much smaller rock, which can be held within your claw as you stand.

In your imagination strike the big rock lightly and visualize it moving away at 100 metres per second. Yes, that's pretty fast.

Now imagine striking the small rock with the same light force and watch this rock move away at 100 metres per second... Can you see it?"

100 metres after 1 second
200 metres after 2 seconds
300 metres after 3 seconds

metres (m) per second (s) = m/s

100 m/s

100 m

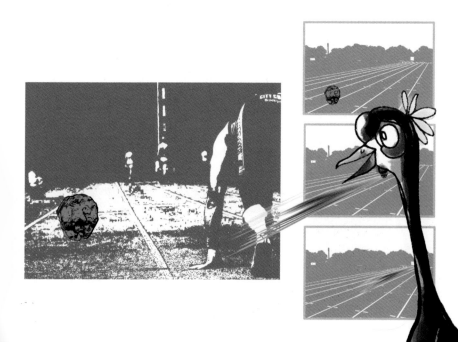

"In One's mindspace anything is possible, the only limits are the Ones that people accept on themselves. These limits, if they exist, can be removed, because the mind has a naturally unlimited capacity...

In One's mindspace ANYTHING is possible.

In the material world of earth objects are governed by many laws (also known as principles **ንጥር**).

If you stood before two rocks like the ones we imagined and applied an equally light force to both of them you'd generally find that the big bolder did not move at all and the small rock moved only a small distance.

If you had the power to force the two rocks to travel at 100 metres per second you would typically find that the bigger rock required a greater force than the smaller rock to get them both to travel at 100 metres per second. This is because the bigger bolder has a greater mass than the smaller one.

Now you're working
with science!

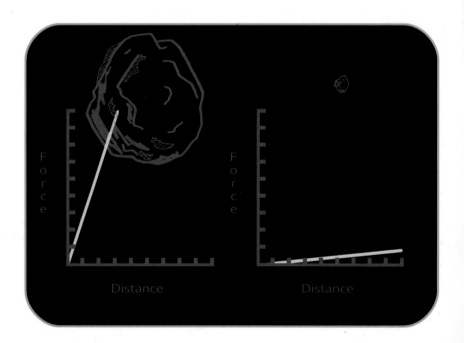

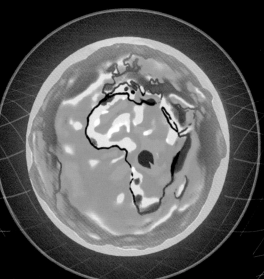

Mass (m) is a
Measure of the amount
of energy-matter (b.r.ha.n :
ch'eh.leh.ma ::) in an object. It is
calculated by establishing balance
in fixed and agreed units of mass.
Unlike **weight**, which is subject to
gravity (a), One's mass remains
constant regardless of where in
the universe One is. By today's
international standards mass is
measured in **grams & kilograms**
(kg). Often we find that people
speak about weight with the units
of grams and kilograms, this is not
correct. Weight is a kind of
"bonding force", a reflection of
curvatures in spacetime and
energy-matter, by international
standards it is measured in
Newtons (N), today's recognized
unit of **force (F)**.

▸ *Object's mass (**m**): 10kg*
▸ *መሬት:: (meh.re.t::)*
  *Earth gravity (**a**): 9.81m/s²*
▸ *"bonding force" (**F**) = 98.10N*

▸ *gravity (a): 23.12m/s²*
▸ *F = 231.20N*

▸ *gravity (a): 8.96m/s²*
▸ *F = 89.60N*

gravity (a): 8.96m/s² ▸
F = 89.60N ▸

KEY: F = m•a

Spacetime

Again from a mysterious place Abit's voice spoke to the young Ones.

Imagine that you are in a place where there are absolutely no things and there is no body else. Even your physical body does not exist.

You are simply conscious of your being...

Imagine now,
how you would describe this space?

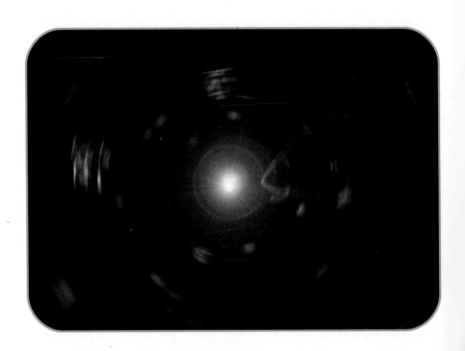

A great feeling of peace came over the trinity as they said softly… "I am… and One is my nature."

Abit spoke again, "Physical space is defined by objects (things/bodies), their locations and the relationship they have with each other. It appears to include distances, areas and three-dimensional capacities (volumes). Today's internationally agreed unit for the measurement of space is the metre, its subunits are centimetres and millimetres.

Interestingly, a metre is defined as:

The length of the path travelled by light in vacuum during a time interval of 1/299,792,458ᵗʰ of a second".

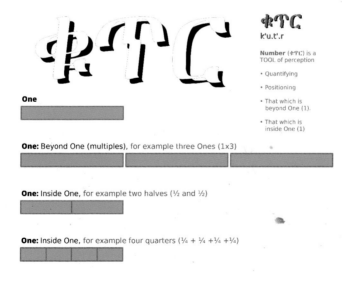

ቁጥር
k'u.t'.r

Number (ቁጥር) is a TOOL of perception

• Quantifying

• Positioning

• That which is beyond One (1).

• That which is inside One (1)

One

One: Beyond One (multiples), for example three Ones (1x3)

One: Inside One, for example two halves (½ and ½)

One: Inside One, for example four quarters (¼ + ¼ +¼ +¼)

This shows a direct relationship between length, light and time. Now young Ones... you've learnt a little about space and a little about light and you even know a little about the invisible darklight...

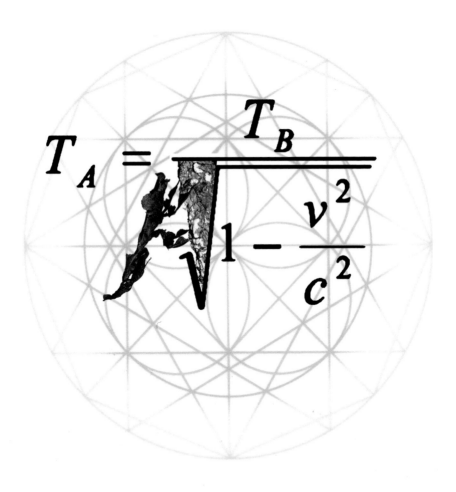

$$T_A = \frac{T_B}{\sqrt{1 - \dfrac{v^2}{c^2}}}$$

What is time?

Can you make time to understand time?

Abit smiled, at what the young Ones did not know.

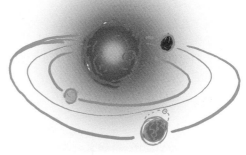

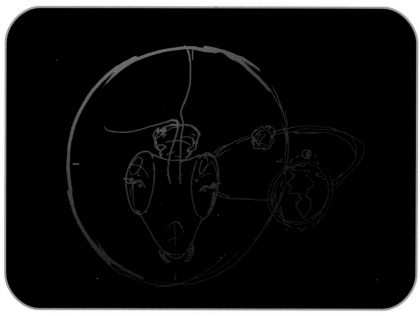

Time is defined by events; singular or cyclical. One's relationship to time is very much affected by One's perception of it.

Examples of nature's cyclical patterns include:

- **days** (the rotation of the planet about its axis),
- **lunar cycles** (the rotation of the moon about the earth – binary planets),
- **years** (annual cycle of the earth around the sun),
- the **replacement of skin** and **other body tissues** within the human body
- and many, many, many more.

Can you think of other cycles that nature expresses?

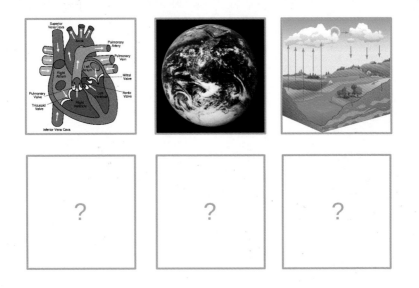

Today the international standard for measuring time
is the 'second'. There are 60 seconds in a minute,
60 minutes in an hour, 24 hours in a day and 365 days
in a year and 25,786 years in a great year (as a basic
idea it is sometimes referenced as 25,920 years,
which is 72 years per degree).

UNLOCK THE MIND and think about this; every 240 seconds (four minutes) the earth travels a distance of 1 degree in its daily rotation about its axis. Degrees are the natural measurement of rotations (cycles) with 360 degrees forming one complete cycle.

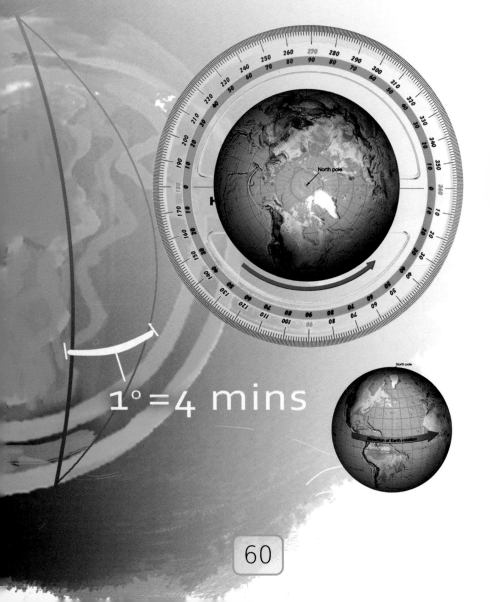

1°=4 mins

60

The question is

No two things can occupy the same space and time, thus, everything that exists has it's own space and it's own time, which means that the each One has a unique **ግዛት** g.za.t.

Are you responsible for your g.za.t? Are you able to respond to the unique needs of your g.za.t?

Now, my children, you have been shown the fundamental principles of the g.za.t, but to really know it you must… experience it.

ሐሺማ፡ተዋጊ፡አሳብ።
ha.shi.ma : teh.wa.gi : a.sa.b ::
(Respect the Warrior Idea).

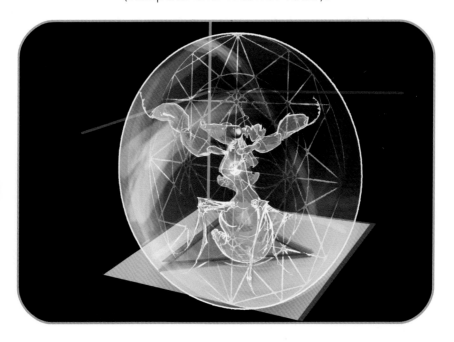

61

When One knows the dimensions of I-Personal
Province, the I will know the answers to these
questions, and with this knowledge the I will have
completed this learning with respect – Hashima.

ha.shi.ma
1111.110100.11001

111111010011001

R E S P E C T
H A S H I M A
ሐ   ሺ.   ማ
15   52   25

1111:110100:11001
MATHEMATICS

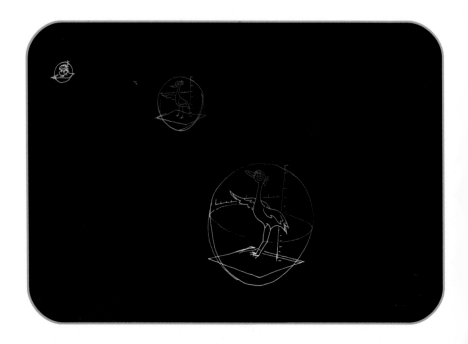

1. Where is the centre of I-Personal Province?
2. What is the weight of I-Personal Province?
3. What is the mass of I-Personal Province?
4. What is the diameter of I-Personal Province?
5. What is the ground space area of I-Personal Province?
6. What is the circumference of I-Personal Province?
7. What is the I-Sphere Volume of I-Personal Province?
8. What vibrates in I-Personal Province?
9. What is the unlimited greatness of I-Personal Province?

Go now and explore I-Personal Province.
It's your birthright to master the g.za.t.

እግዚር : ይምስጋን:: ሐሺማ : ተዋጊ : አሳብ::
ur.g.z.r : yi.m.s.ga.n :: ha.shi.ma : teh.wa.gi : a.sa.b::

Way out

The three young Winchi had greatly enjoyed all of this magical inner world, then, as if shaking off water, they shook themselves back to the present moment...

"Wow!" One said. "How did you get this well inside your head? It's a beautiful place."

Abit did not answer the question, looking deep into the Winchi birds' eyes, the mantid (Abit) just reminded the young Ones of their commitment. Then Abit spoke with a serious tone "This is a special thing, which is hard to explain, even to the greatness of your flight full brains. Reflect on what you have learnt and what you know. Watch carefully as your province grows."

On the way back to the Winchi family's special gathering grounds the young Ones met a friend and after a time the youngest of the Winchi said to him

"I'm not going to tell anyone."

So the friend said, "What aren't you going to tell anyone?"

In a rush of excitement the young One spurted "I'm not going to tell anyone that Abit has a beautiful well inside her head".

As quickly as she had said it they all realized that she wasn't supposed to tell. Anyway, she had seen so much that she really didn't know how to explain it or even what else to say. The young bird said no more, trying to pretend that what she had said wasn't really very important.

The friend went and told another friend "Did you know that Abit has a well inside her head." Then that friend went and told another friend "Did you hear about Abit? She's not well in the head." By the time the secret had got around it had completely changed.

Now, even the wind was whispering
the distorted secret (blow out)
"Abit", (blow in) "is not well",
(blow out) "in the head."

ትንፋሽ : አዘዝ ::
t.n.fa.sh : ah.zeh.zeh ::

Four types of Breath Command

ኔን:: en::
equal breath in,
equal breath out.

ካ:: ka::
utterance with
emotional content
(singing, poetry, chant etc).

ዖም:: om::
peace.

ኢ:: i::
determination.

Drums

The young One's friend's friend's friend found herself roosting in an Eboni tree, singing.

" Abit's not well in the head.
Abit's not well in the head."

She sang for a long time, and then when she had left the tree a local man named Ahmar Tahamaki passed.

He was a very good drummer from a nearby village and on that day he had decided to make some new drums. As he passed, he took a special liking to this same beautiful Eboni tree that the young One's friend's friend's friend was sitting in, singing.

	om-i-i-om			
Drummer1:	1000110011011	1101100		1101100100011 0011011

	om			
Drummer2:	1000110011011	1000110011011		1000110011011

	i			
Drummer3:		1101100	1101100	1101100

70

The man cut the tree and brought it back to his village where he made four very beautiful drums. On Saturday he invited all of his friends around to enjoy them.

So the drums played and the people all had a great time. In this age the people where so peaceful that the birds freely joined in their gatherings and enjoyment.

Play the ዖግ ለ (Om I) drum pattern and sing along:
10001100.11011;[2s pause] 1101100;[2s pause]
1101100;[1s pause]10001100.11011;;[2s pause & repeat]

Drums are amazing
Instruments!

The drums were playing
a response to the song that
the young One's friend's
friend's friend was singing as
she sat in the Eboni tree.

" Abit's not well in the head.
Abit's not well in the head."

Now the people and Winchi gathered, enjoying the rhythm of the music so much that they danced and sang for hours.

የም ኢ ጤና ይስጥልኝ፦ ኢ የም ጤና ይስጥልኝ፦
om i t'ena yist'lng. i om t'ena yist'lng.

የም ኢ ጤና ይስጥልኝ፦ ኢ የም ጤና ይስጥልኝ፦
om i t'ena yist'lng. i om t'ena yist'lng.

Play the የም ኢ (Om I) drum pattern and sing along:

10001100.11011.[2s pause] 1101100.[2s pause]
1101100.[1s pause]10001100.11011.[2s pause & repeat]

Now the rhythm, the song and the dancing were so sweet that thousands started travelling to Abit's place, singing and dancing, as they went.

Hidden view

From afar, Abit with her excellent sense and hearing heard all the community coming. she heard the message in the wind, she heard their song and she knew exactly what the drums' rhythm was saying.

She thought to herself "hmmm! Those young Ones said they would not tell... now the whole community wants to enter my g.za.t."

Abit decided to hide in a very tall Baobab tree. She blended so well with the colours of the tree that she became invisible.

When the community arrived at Abit's place they found it empty. The children and the young Winchi missed her VERY much and so they sang.

ያም ኪ ጤና ይስጥልኝ:: ኪ ያም ጤና ይስጥልኝ::
om i t'ena yist'lng. i om t'ena yist'lng.

ያም ኪ ጤና ይስጥልኝ:: ኪ ያም ጤና ይስጥልኝ::
om i t'ena yist'lng. i om t'ena yist'lng.

"Abit! Abit! They called. "Come back!" "We're not going to tell anyone else that you're not well in the head. Come back!", but she never did.

They searched high and low for Abit but they never found her. Up to this day they still haven't seen her again.

High, high, high up in the Baobab tree,
Abit shook her head "እንዴ! (ur.n.de!) That child!"

Abit smiled, "I just knew they'd tell my secret, but I do
love it when young Ones show interest in learning.
እግዚር ይምስጋን:: ur.g.z.r : yi.m.s.ga.n ::"

Gently rocking from side to side, Abit looked into the
community with great depth, as they passed each day.

Time passed and then, one beautiful day, Abit saw the three young Winchi again!

They were singing and playing just below the Baobab tree, so Abit watched carefully.

With the wisdom of the ancients Abit rocked from side to side as she knew, just from the way they played and the freedom of their harmonious singing, that they were now able to answer all the questions correctly.

Even though she had not forgotten the broken word, Abit was relaxed as she enjoyed the singing, which was sweetness to the ear.

ያም ኢ ጤና ይስጥልኝ፨ ኢ ያም ጤና ይስጥልኝ፨
om i t'ena yist'lng. i om t'ena yist'lng.

ያም ኢ ጤና ይስጥልኝ፨ ኢ ያም ጤና ይስጥልኝ፨
om i t'ena yist'lng. i om t'ena yist'lng.

Play the ያም ኢ (Om I) drum pattern and sing along:

10001100.11011.[2s pause] 1101100.[2s pause]
1101100.[1s pause]10001100.11011.[2s pause & repeat]

The End
...is always a beginning..

እግዝር ይምስጋን፨ ሐሺማ ተዋጊ አሳብ፨

A creative allegory

The essence of space and life:
Meta & Quantum – Physics & Maths

An allegory is a story, poem, or picture that can be interpreted to reveal a hidden meaning, they are wonderful vehicles for learning. Journeying with a good story greatly enhances One's ability to question and visualise. This is especially true when studying dynamics which are beyond our everyday awareness. We must remember that enhanced visualisation is the great prize of science and maths practice.

The story of **Abit's Secret** forms the basis of a special performance which is periodically presented by Schools of Unified Learning's honourable learning community, whilst sharing progress in the unified approach to learning; የጥምር፡ዕውቀት፦ *yeht'mr urwuk'eht*, (unifiedknowledge).

It makes sense that a creature as ancient and wise as አቢት Abit (the Praying Mantis) is the focus for exploring One's outer and inner space (ግዛት)- She makes the most amazing 'instar' (moult) lifecycle transformations, a great metaphor for internal and external environmental change.

In the unfolding drama of Abit's Secret we find ourselves in the 'well' water of Abit's head! Water is an important basis of life. It is a key substance in all living things and so within it we find many special patterns, which provide great metaphors for the primal life-field. Within the story this "field" is called ብርሃን፡ጨለማ፦ 'b.r.ha.n : ch'eh.leh.ma', 'darklight' or the 'light without light', the use of this creative label enables us to bring together and wield the embedded ideas with a more intuitive ease.

Enjoy the story and develop your ability to express the Self as the ዊንቺ Winchi (African Crowned Crane) and አቢት Abit (African Dead Leaf Mantis). With these two beautiful warrior guides we're sure to become both curious and fearless enough to explore the deepest natures of space and the response-ability it inspires.

All this and more is explored through these kinds of unifiedknowledge (yeht'mr urwuk'eht) dramas.

Importantly, we recognise:

- The underlying science and maths of the **ግዛት** gzat (space, One's province)
- The natural unity of art and mathematics
- The value of **የጥምር፡ዕውቀት፡፡** (yeht'mr urwuk'eht, unifiedknowledge approaches to learning)
- The presence of duality

'Land' and 'Air' (matter and energy) can be shown to have particular patterns that are themselves determined by natural laws (underlying principles). Minds' great power and patterns are best realised as One strives for well-being and continuous self-perfection (self-refinement).

If we conceive of the great life-field as a 'province' then it becomes a space we are responsible for and are more aware in. This has far-reaching implications, therefore we have an obligation to **overstand** (not just understand) the various ways its harmonies can be established and maintained. As a microcosm of the total life-field we are more tangibly responsible for our 'personal province' and so grow in knowledge of its intimate relationship to the whole. Consciousness and the perception of One's province is not stagnant (in a healthy being), it expands, until we become truly aware of responsibility for (and influence in) One's universal province (**ግዛት**).

As an important, life-long-learning we come to realise that this growth is also expressed through the 'science' and 'mathematics' of 'dance' movement, unified in one (learning) realisation – yeht'mr urwuk'eht (የጥምር:ዕሙቀት::).

Abit's Secret – Overstanding the Warrior's Province forms a foundational part of our approach to this learning. Through the repeated study of this story and its related insights, disciplines and ዳንኪራ ተዋጊ Dankira Tehwagi (Warrior Dance) skills, learners gain an essential and profound grasp of space - One's Province (gzat). This, along with our course entitled **Transformations of Winchi**, provides a basic foundation to higher learning which reaffirms correct standards for our young people, families and communities.

Do look out for:

- The expressive performance of Abit (the Praying Mantis, fire & earth) and Winchi (the Crane, water and air).
- The demonstration of the 5 important shapes expressed as movement, numbers and in እጎማ ngoma (Dankira Tehwagi free play warrior dance).
- The way our "binary" style drumming is used to express mathematical vibration; language and music.
- Insights you personally gain and how you feel during and after the show or reading the story.

Movements towards overstanding.

What is learning?

Learning is about acquiring (absorbing/realising) new knowledge, patterns of thought, behaviours, skills, values, preferences and understanding and/or overstanding and often involves synthesising different types of experience and information.

The ability to learn is possessed by humans, animals and in a virtual sense, by some machines.

It could be said that human beings are always learning, because on a subtle (super-conscious) level we are constantly taking in ambient information and having it inform our being. That aside, the common sense idea of learning is related to **determined** acts of study, education or practice.

In this learning One must be 'willing to learn'. This willingness connects and strengthens One's interest in the area of study and with it One acquires the right attitude for learning. Interest and attitude are two additional keywords that must be overstood. Losing interest and having the wrong attitude are major obstacles to learning.

DETERMINED LEARNING typically involves One making progress over time and tends to follow a definable learning curve (or gradient). In previewing and defining the learning curve we are interested in knowing the key stages, points and periods along the curve.

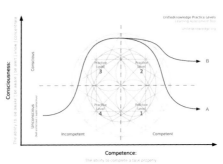

Understanding the Warrior's Province:

In the martial-cultural arts practice of **ዳንኪራ ተዋጊ** Dankira Tehwagi the **የተዋጊ ግዛት** Warrior's Province is "a region of space that One perceives as their responsibility". Initially, we are concerned with our personal space (**I-Personal Province**) , which encompasses One's body and surrounding area. The realisation of I-Personal Province provides a key foundation as One begins to study and apply One's knowledge of patterns (mathematics).

This Unifiedknowledge learning resource guides us through some of the key terms and principles of Dankira Tehwagi. Thereafter we look at five important shapes and forms. As you study these, you will realise just how prominent these shapes are in our day-to-day lives. Next, we grasp the basic ideas of energy-matter, space and time. Now we're ready to start defining I-Province, here we begin with I-Personal Province but ultimately we become aware of I-Universal Province (the total life-field). Through the study of the 'small', we can learn about the 'large' – as above so below. This defining process explores dimensions, centres, weight, mass, lengths, areas and volumes.

Having defined I-Personal Province One is better able to visualise it. This process of building deeper perception reveals that I-Province is vibrating; it has a pulse… well, several in fact. However, the fundamental nature of a pulse brings us into the subject of binary (counting with 1's and 0's) and that brings us neatly into the power of the Drum, where we discover that our natural patterns (mathematics) make music. This learning resource concludes with an introduction to Breath Command (**ትንፋሽ:ከዘዘ**:: t.n fa.sh:ah.zeh.zeh::), which is the beginning of another vital insight; mind-breath-body harmonisation.

Dance and live free in the knowledge of One's infinite capacity to create in (and with) the great life-field.

The principles revealed with the aid of this learning resource can be either simplified or enhanced, which means that they can be shared from early years right throughout the generations.
The story can serve as an excellent beginning or as a natural complement to many important learning objectives.

For example we can:

1) Learn how to explain and illustrate the basic idea of ሒሳብ (hi.sa.b) mathematics.
2) Learn the approach of an Advanced Learner (አስተማሪ a.s.teh.ma.ri); ሐሺማ ha.shi.ma (Respect), ታጀባ ta.ja.ba (an advanced learning model) and መሠረታዊ:ሒሳብ:: meh.seh.reh.ta.wi : hah.sa.b :: (the basic idea).
3) Learn about the five important shapes related to I-personal Province (የተዋጊ ግዛት). To learn about the nature, related numbers and ways of expressing them through our dance movements (triangles, squares, circles, cubes and spheres).
4) Come to greatly value the precursors to building shape and form; points, lines, curves and spirals.
5) Learn the *mehsehrehtawi hahsab* of energy-matter (vibration patterns) and the space, time and relationship of this to One's Personal Province.
6) Learn how to define, measure and visualise I-personal province: it's Centre, Diameter, Weight, Mass, Volume, Ground Space Area, Circumference and Greatness.
7) Learn to count with Nought (0) and One (1) and understand the importance of nature's pulse: The Binary Number Base System.
8) Learn the *mehsehrehtawi hahsab* of Binary Drumming; a practice that brings together music, language, maths, unity and concentration development into one form.
9) Enhance One's values of ትንፋሽ:ኣዘዘ::t.n.fa.sh : ah.zeh.zeh :: (*Tnfash Ahzehzeh* / Breath Command) – The pulse of One's own Province.

Enjoy the great learning.

Answering the questions

What are the dimensions of I-Personal Province?
Centre, Weight, Mass, Diameter, Ground Space Area, Circumference, I-Sphere Volume & Greatness

Land:

Centre:	*Solar Plexus*	
Weight:	*Mass times Gravity*	*N*
Mass:	*Weight divided by Gravity*	*kg*
Head to Toe Height:		*cm*
Hands High Height:	*Used as Diameter (cm)*	*cm*
Arm Span:		*cm*
Area of Ground Space:	*Pi (3.14) times the Radius Squared*	*cm²* · *m²*
Circumference of Ground Space:	*Pi (3.14) times the Diameter*	*cm* · *m*

Air:

I-Sphere: One's personal atmosphere; Volume of air space:	$V = (4 Pi/3)r3$ $V = (Pi/6)d3$	*cm³* · *m³*

Mind:

Number:	*One*
Capacity of the Mind:	*Unlimited*
Guiding Principles:	*Oneness (unity)*
	Peace
	Power
	Wisdom
	Will
	Balance
	Justice
	Intellect
	Imagination
	Devotion (faith)
	Worldliness

Lengths of I-Personal Province (*a way to enhance visualisation*)

Lengths are important when looking at the landspace of I-Personal Province – One's body and the ground upon which One stands or rests. When the key lengths have been measured One is able to calculate Areas and Volumes associated to I-Personal Province. There are many lengths that One should study for example the length of One's; feet, walking stride, height, waist, chest, legs, hand spans etc.

Beginning with the meh.seh.reh.ta.wi : hah.sa.b :: One should initially measure three key lengths. They are:

- **Head to Toe Height:**
  A vertical measurement from the floor (feet) directly up to the length level with the top of One's head.

- **Hands High Height**
  A vertical measurement from the floor (feet) directly up to the length level with the tips of One's fingers after the arm and hands have been raised directly above the head to the greatest natural extent.

- **Arm Span:**
  A horizontal measurement from the fingertips of the left hand directly to the finger tips of the right hand. The hands should be extended at shoulder level, horizontally to their greatest natural outward extension.

With younger people these measurements should be reassessed every three, four or six months, this forms a good exercise in learning to monitor One's growth and thus the natural and physical expansion of I-Personal Province.

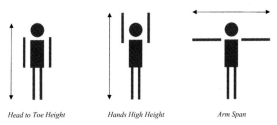

Head to Toe Height   Hands High Height   Arm Span

Remember: Mathematics is the study and application of patterns.

The Area of I-Personal Province's Ground Space

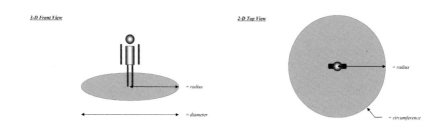

3-D Front View

2-D Top View

= radius

= diameter

= radius

= circumference

I-Personal Province has a **Ground Space Area**. This takes a circular form, which is centred by One's body (the feet when standing, the solar plexus when lying horizontally). The diameter is defined by the length of the Hands High Height. Below is the key background information that One needs to know to calculate One's Ground Space Area and Circumference.

- The **diameter** is double (twice, two times) the size of the radius, and goes right across the circle through its centre.

- The **radius** always begins at the circles centre and radiates outwards (halfway across the circle) to its edge (perimeter), which in a circle is called the **circumference**.

- **Pi** (π) is an ordinary number that has a special relationship to circles. Depending to the level of accuracy required its value is expressed as; 3, 3.14 or 3.142.

- The **circumference** = Pi x Diameter,
  which is typically expressed as $C = pi \times d$

- The **area** = **pi x radius squared**
  which is typically expressed as $A = Pi \times r^2$
  (Radius² = radius squared)

Drum patterns and our song

Nature's Pulse, the Drum and Binary Number Base

Now that we have defined the dimensions of I-Personal Province we are better able to visualise it. Every part of I-Province vibrates, which means that we live in and are a living orchestra of rhythmic cycles – Nature's pulse. The mehsehrehtawi hahsab of vibrations is that they express a high and low or what might be viewed as an in and out. Essentially a vibration expresses duality – two opposing polarities that make up a whole.

Binary Number Base Mathematics

If I gave you sets of red balls and blue balls and asked you to do arithmetic with them using one colour for one number value and the other for another number value (two values only) I would be asking you to do binary arithmetic.

Binary is from the Latin binarius, which means doing it with two together (bini + ary)

At first sight, it may seem that you cannot count higher than two. However, this is not so.

In our popular everyday counting, we have only ten digits (0 to 9), but, by putting them in different places, we can carry on counting until we stop with exhaustion.

We can do the same with two balls or two digits; 1's and 0's.

Binary Number Base:
Counting Chart / Binary Drum Patterns

2^9	2^8	2^7	2^6	2^5	2^4	2^3	2^2	2^1	2^0	Decimal
512	256	128	64	32	16	8	4	2	1	Decimal
									0	0
									1	1
								1	0	2
								1	1	3
							1	0	0	4
							1	0	1	5
							1	1	0	6
							1	1	1	7
						1	0	0	0	8
						1	0	0	1	9
						1	0	1	0	10
						1	0	1	1	11
						1	1	0	0	12
						1	1	0	1	13
						1	1	1	0	14
						1	1	1	1	15
					1	0	0	0	0	16
					1	0	0	0	1	17
					1	0	0	1	0	18
					1	0	0	1	1	19
					1	0	1	0	0	20
					1	0	1	0	1	21
					1	0	1	1	0	22
					1	0	1	1	1	23
					1	1	0	0	0	24
					1	1	0	0	1	25
					1	1	0	1	0	26
					1	1	0	1	1	27
					1	1	1	0	0	28
					1	1	1	0	1	29
					1	1	1	1	0	30
					1	1	1	1	1	31
				1	0	0	0	0	0	32

Binary Drum Patterns

The drum is truly a beautiful instrument and tool. እግዚር ይምስጋን:: ሐሺማ ተዋጊ አሳብ:: (ur.g.z.r : yi.m.s.ga.n :: ha.shi.ma : teh.wa.gi : a.sa.b ::) Its vibrations can bring peace, happiness, upliftment, enlightenment, healing and discipline. As an ancient African musical instrument, it can elevate One's creativity in profound ways. Collective drumming provides a great forum for the study and practice of unity.

The drum gives a natural analogy to One's heartbeat, breathing, hearing, walking, dancing and numerous other functions and expressions of life. It is due the highest hashima (respect).

The Binary Drum practice a unique innovation of **Schools Of Unified Learning (SOUL)**. Its patterns and principles form an excellent way of introducing drumming and the Binary Base Number System to both children and adults.

Review the Chart above and explore the patterns by allowing the bass (middle) of the drum to be represented by the 0's and the tone (edge) of the drum to be represented by the 1's. It is best to begin by drumming with One's own body. Let light open hand slaps to the thighs be the 0's and hands clapped together be the 1's. For example:

1001 (which is binary for the decimal number nine) becomes Clap, Slap, Slap, Clap with the body and Tone, Bass, Bass, Tone on the drum.

Now have a look at this chart.

These charts and other bonus resources are available here:

web: unifiedknowledge.org/links/abitsextras

ዕውቀት ብርሃን ነው !

ሀ	ሁ	ሂ	ሃ	ሄ	ህ	ሆ
ለ	ሉ	ሊ	ላ	ሌ	ል	ሎ
ሐ	ሑ	ሒ	ሓ	ሔ	ሕ	ሖ
መ	ሙ	ሚ	ማ	ሜ	ም	ሞ
ሠ	ሡ	ሢ	ሣ	ሤ	ሥ	ሦ
ረ	ሩ	ሪ	ራ	ሬ	ር	ሮ
ሰ	ሱ	ሲ	ሳ	ሴ	ስ	ሶ
ሸ	ሹ	ሺ	ሻ	ሼ	ሽ	ሾ
ቀ	ቁ	ቂ	ቃ	ቄ	ቅ	ቆ
በ	ቡ	ቢ	ባ	ቤ	ብ	ቦ
ተ	ቱ	ቲ	ታ	ቴ	ት	ቶ
ቸ	ቹ	ቺ	ቻ	ቼ	ች	ቾ
ኀ	ኁ	ኂ	ኃ	ኄ	ኅ	ኆ
ነ	ኑ	ኒ	ና	ኔ	ን	ኖ
ኘ	ኙ	ኚ	ኛ	ኜ	ኝ	ኞ
አ	ኡ	ኢ	ኣ	ኤ	እ	ኦ
ከ	ኩ	ኪ	ካ	ኬ	ክ	ኮ
ኸ	ኹ	ኺ	ኻ	ኼ	ኽ	ኾ
ወ	ዉ	ዊ	ዋ	ዌ	ው	ዎ
ዐ	ዑ	ዒ	ዓ	ዔ	ዕ	ዖ
ዘ	ዙ	ዚ	ዛ	ዜ	ዝ	ዞ
ዠ	ዡ	ዢ	ዣ	ዤ	ዥ	ዦ
የ	ዩ	ዪ	ያ	ዬ	ይ	ዮ
ደ	ዱ	ዲ	ዳ	ዴ	ድ	ዶ
ጀ	ጁ	ጂ	ጃ	ጄ	ጅ	ጆ
ገ	ጉ	ጊ	ጋ	ጌ	ግ	ጎ
ጠ	ጡ	ጢ	ጣ	ጤ	ጥ	ጦ
ጨ	ጩ	ጪ	ጫ	ጬ	ጭ	ጮ
ጰ	ጱ	ጲ	ጳ	ጴ	ጵ	ጶ
ጸ	ጹ	ጺ	ጻ	ጼ	ጽ	ጾ
ፀ	ፁ	ፂ	ፃ	ፄ	ፅ	ፆ
ፈ	ፉ	ፊ	ፋ	ፌ	ፍ	ፎ
ፐ	ፑ	ፒ	ፓ	ፔ	ፕ	ፖ

የግዕምር ዕውቀት
ግ ዕ ክ ሳ ት

SOUL has taken this system very far, we connect it to the Ethiopian Fidel (syllabary / alphabet) by converting each fidel (letter) into its ordinal number value. **ሀ** Hah is 1 like A is 1, **ሁ** Hu is 2 like B is 2, **ሂ** Hi is 3 like C is 3, and so on. This then allows us to turn any word from most languages of the world into a drum pattern. In Abit's Secret the anthem (zema / chant / song) goes:

ዖም ኢ ጤና ይስጥልኝ:: ኢ ዖም ጤና ይስጥልኝ::
ዖም ኢ ጤና ይስጥልኝ:: ኢ ዖም ጤና ይስጥልኝ::
om i t'ena yist'lng. i om t'ena yist'lng.
om i t'ena yist'lng. i om t'ena yist'lng.

1100

ዖም "Om" is a breath of **peace**, **ኢ** "I" (sounded as and elongated 'ee') is a breath of **determination** and t'ena yist'lgn means 'give thanks for health' and is commonly used as a general greeting..

So we turn the **ዖም ኢ** (om i) of this African utterance into its number form by converting each fidel into its ordinal number value:

ዖም:ኢ becomes
140.27:108 which is then converted into its binary form and is this
10001100.11011:1101100:

One now have the foundational key information to develop your Binary Drumming practice. Work in groups as often as possible and enjoy making music and talking with the drum! Remember you can (and should) start doing this as a clapping exercise. You'll be pleased to note that additional courses and resources are available to help advance in practice. The above is a very concise introduction to get Ones moving.
(see page 99)

clap = 1   slap = 0

Glossary of Key words and terms

albo, አልቦ, empty, zero

Abit, አቢት a.bi.t:: 1) praying mantis (insect), 2) African Dead Leaf Mantis.

airspace, 1) air/gases, 2) energy, 3) areas and volume, 4) see ግዛት

allegory, a story, poem, or picture which can be interpreted to reveal a hidden meaning, typically a moral or political one.

Amharic. አማርኛ ah.ma.r.nga the official language of Ethiopia, a Semitic language descended from Ge'ez ግዕዝ g.ur.z and spoken by about 9 million people.

Astehmari Batekun, Principal teacher at Schools Of Unified Learning (SOUL). Twitter: @astehmari, https://uk.linkedin.com/in/astehmaribatekun

atomic elements, The word atom is derived from the word atom and atum which means indivisible. Atoms are composed of three type of particles (atomic elements): protons, neutrons, and electron

axion, A starting point of reasoning conceived as a premise / postulate so evident as to be accepted as true without controversy.

balance, an even distribution of weight enabling someone or something to remain upright and steady.

baobab tree, a bombacaceous tree, Adansonia digitata, native to Africa, that has a very thick trunk, large white flowers, and a gourdlike fruit with an edible pulp

binary drumming, unique drumming system used in SOUL and Unifiedknowledge practice that connects number, music and language creativity.

birthright, a particular right of possession or privilege a person has from birth. A natural or moral right, possessed by everyone.

brhan ch'ehlehma, see ብርሃን:ጨለማ::

bonding forces forces of attraction or repulsion which act between neighbouring particles such as atoms, molecules or ions.

circle, a round plane figure whose boundary (the circumference) consists of points equidistant from a fixed point (the centre).

circumference, the enclosing boundary of a curved geometric figure, especially a circle.

competent, having the necessary ability, knowledge, or skill to do something properly / successfully.

conscious / consciousness, the state of being awake, aware, alert, knowledgeable and expressing concentration of and responsive to one's surrounding and internal environments.

cube, a symmetrical three-dimensional shape, either solid or hollow, contained by six equal squares.

Dankira Tehwagi, Warrior Dance of a specific pattern. Mind-breath-body harmonisation practice and African martial-cultural art-science.

Darklight, see ብርሃን:ጨለማ::

density, the degree of compactness of a substance.

diameter, a straight line passing from side to side through the centre of a body or figure, especially a circle or sphere.

dimensions, an aspect or feature of a situation.

duality, two states, two poles, both of which arise from an apparent division of unity. ie. wave-particle, negative-positive, inner-outer space, electric-magnetic fields etc.

eboni tree / ebony tree, Ebony is a dense black wood, most commonly yielded by several different species in the genus Diospyros. Ebony is dense enough to sink in water. It is finely-textured and has a very smooth beautiful finish when polished,

electrons, the electron is a subatomic particle with a negative elementary electric charge.

elements, an essential or characteristic part of something abstract.

energy, In physics, energy is a property of objects which can be transferred to other objects or converted into different forms, but cannot be created or destroyed.

fire, a process in which substances combine chemically with oxygen from the air and typically give out bright light, heat, and smoke; combustion or burning.

force, In physics, a force is any interaction that, when unopposed, will change the motion of an object. In other words, a force can cause an object with mass to change its velocity (which includes to begin moving from a state of rest), i.e., to accelerate. Force can also be described by intuitive concepts such as a push or a pull.

gzat, also g.za.t, see ግዛት

gas, an air-like fluid substance which expands freely to fill any space available, irrespective of its quantity.

gravity or gravitation, a natural phenomenon by which all things appear to attract one another including stars, planets, galaxies, other beings and even light and sub-atomic particles.

ground space area, a conceptual aspect of I-personal-province, see page 88.

hashima, respect, see ሐሺማ

harmony, "joint, agreement, concord" is the blend of sounds (or other factors) in such a manner that the overall sound (experience) is enhanced. It has therefore the character of 'emergence', where the enjoyed sum is greater than the parts.

health, a state of physical, mental, and social well-being (vibrant, creative, perceptive, determined and growing) accompanied by a freedom from illness, disease or pain. Health can be viewed as a type of harmony.

i, 1) one's self, 2) "i" is a type of breathing practice which carries the extended sound "ee" and develops will / determination.

Idea, አሳብ:: (ah.sa.b::), 1) A private or public mental object(ive), 2) A mental conception representing something. 3) The "idea" contains its object(ive)'s character(istics) and purpose, thus an idea is intentional, connecting principle (rule) to visionary form. 4) Ideas prove One's profound consciousness. 5) Ideas are motivational; the directors of energy.

i-sphere volume, spherical space of one's personal space.

international standard, (French: Système International d'Unités, SI) is the modern form of the metric system (eurocentric), it comprises a coherent and internationally agreed system of seven "base" units of measurement plus their derivatives

Kush, Africa, focally the ancient Nile valley civilisations (Ethiopia, Egypt Sudan and surrounding regions)

landspace, 1) earth, 2) matter, 3) points and lines, 4) see ግዛት.

laws, 1) generally a system of rules that are enforced through human social institutions to govern behaviour. 2) natural principles (ንጥር nt'r)

line, 1) the properties of lines are determined by the axioms which refer to them, it is a _primitive notion_. The notion of a line or straight line is an idealization concept to help define objects that appear straight (i.e., appear to have no curvature). 2) a line is a straight one-dimensional figure having no thickness and extending infinitely in both directions

liquid, having a consistency like that of water or oil, i.e., flowing freely but of constant volume.

mass, the quantity of matter that a body contains, as measured by its acceleration under a given force or by the force exerted on it by a gravitational field.

master, 1) acquire complete knowledge or skill in (a subject, technique, or art), 2) having or showing very great skill or proficiency.

material world, refers to the physical aspects of nature in the broadest sense, being local or universal.

mathematics, is the study and application of patterns.

matrix, a substance, situation, or environment in which something has its origin.

matter, physical substance in general, as distinct from mind and spirit; (in physics) that which occupies space and possesses rest mass, especially as distinct from energy.

measure (መዘን meh.zeh.neh), a process of comparing relative size.

metre, said to be and agreed fundamental unit of length in the metric system (see international standard, eurocentric).

microcosm, a community, place, or situation regarded as encapsulating in miniature the characteristics of something much larger.

mind. the faculty of consciousness, thought, feeling, will and creativity. see ግዛት

mindspace, see ግዛት

molecules,   a group of atoms bonded together, representing the smallest fundamental unit of a chemical compound that can take part in a chemical reaction.

natural laws (underlying principles), 1) a body of unchanging moral principles regarded as a basis for all human conduct. 2) an observable law/principle relating to natural phenomena.

negative qualities, an axiom that works with "positive qualities" and "neutral qualities" to express the status of a unit (ie, an atom, molecule, person etc) or system. There are dynamics of attraction and repulsion (powers) that can be harness as units appear to oscillate their states. Units typically appear to "seek" harmony.

neutrons, a subatomic particle of about the same mass as a proton but without an electric charge.

newtons, the name given to the international standard unit of force. it is equal to the force that would give a mass of one kilogram an acceleration of one metre per second per second. see international standards

ngoma, free play martial (warrior) dance of Dankira Tehwagi (& Kazimba Ngoma). African dance movements and gestures that evolve towards harmony and complete freedom of expression.

number, 1) is a tool of perception, 2) an arithmetical value, expressed by a word, symbol, or figure, representing a particular quantity and used in counting and making calculations.

om, a type of breathing discipline related to the development of peace. see ትንፋሽአዘዘ::

overrstanding, in unifiedknowledge practice it is said that one should not "understand" or stand under an idea; when they absorb, correctly perceive and realise an idea (its core and related principles/laws) they "overstand" it and thus one becomes creative. if you can simply use something or do a job without grasp of its core principles, you understand and memorize enough to act. in order to innovate, redesign, be creative, you must overstand. understanding can enable one to drive the car, but overstanding builds it, (or replaces it with something better).

patterns, 1) a regular and intelligible form or sequence discernible in the way in which something happens or is done. 2) a repeated design, shape, form etc.

perceptions, the ability to come to know through one's senses

point, 1) the place one puts one's consciousness, 2) a point is an exact position or location on a plane surface. it is important to overstand that a point is not a thing, but a place. we indicate the position of a point by placing a dot with a pencil. this dot may have a diameter of, say, 0.2mm, but a point has no size. no matter how far you zoomed in, it would still have no width. since a point is a place, not a thing, it has no dimensions.

positive qualities, see negative qualities

power, 1) the ability or capacity to complete a task activity. 2) strength, vigour, force or effectiveness. 3) a person or group exercising control or influence. 4) physics; a measure of the rate of doing work, expressed as 'work done per unit of time'. 5) converting energy from one form to another.

principles, see natural law.

protons, a proton is a subatomic particle found in the nucleus of every atom. the particle has a positive electrical charge, equal and opposite to that of the electron.

ratio, a rule of relationship; parts to each other and parts to the whole.

Schools Of Unified Learning (SOUL), foundation of unifiedknowledge practice.
twitter: @uLearnNaturally,
web: www.unifiedknowledge.org
web: www.youtube.com/unifiedknowledge
web: www.abundancecentre.org

shape, a specific form, a particular condition, the outline of something you can perceive.

solid, of definite shape and volume; not liquid or gaseous.

sphere, a ball shape where the surface is the same distance from the centre at all points.

spiral, a curve on a plane that winds around a fixed centre point at a continuously increasing or decreasing distance from the point.

square, 1) a plane figure (shape) having four equal sides. 2) in maths, the product obtained when a number or quantity is multiplied by itself: 49 is the square of 7.

t'ena yist'lgn see ጤና : ይስጥልኝ ::

Tehwagi Asab, see ተዋጊ አሳብ::

three dimensional, relating to Three-dimensional space (also: 3D) is a geometric three-parameter modelling tool for perception of the physical universe (without considering time) in which all known matter exists. These "three dimensions" can be labelled by a combination of three chosen from the terms length, width, height, depth, and breadth.

time, a point or period of a natural (or artificial) rhythmic cycle typically used in the reckoning (measure for knowledge) of events' relationships in relative space.

Transformations of Winchi, a course and SOUL school workshop using dance (Dankira Tehwagi) to explore and learn the maths ideas related to geometric transformation.

triangle,the plane figure (shape) formed by connecting three points not in a straight line by straight line segments; a three-sided polygon.

trinity, A group consisting of three closely related members.

Unifiedknowledge, see የፒፖር:ዕውቀት::

universal, Of, relating to, or affecting the entire universe: the universal laws of physics.

vibrates, 1) To move back and forth or to and fro, especially rhythmically and rapidly, 2) To produce a sound; resonate.

visualize, To form a mental image of; visualisation is a powerful reason and mechanism for learning maths (the study and application of patterns). It may start with noticing and describing, but it always involves imagination and prediction.

volume, The amount of space occupied by a three-dimensional object or region of space, expressed in cubic units.

water, A clear, colourless, odourless, and tasteless liquid, H_2O, essential for most plant and animal life and the most widely used of all solvents. Freezing point 0°C (32°F); boiling point 100°C (212°F);

Winchi, ዊንቺ wi.n.chi:: 1) cranes (birds), 2) African Crowned Crane.

አንድነት:: ah.n.d.neh.t::, unity

አንዴ:: ur.n.de:: an expression of being greatly impressed

ሐሺማ ha(h).shi.ma (heshima) is a swahili word that within our community is imbued with a very profound depth. Hashima directly means respect. The value of respect is universally understood amongst all people of the world, thus it's expression is a universal language. From an African place of being we recognise that respect calls on gratitude, which is rightly shown at the beginning and end of all matters of importance. Thus we give thanks. Hashima is appreciation, honour and admiration. That which One respects is well thought of. Hashima is due to everyone, everything and every experience as all come into being via higher orders. At the heart of hashima is maat; Where hashima is lacking... there is danger.

ማኣት ma.a.t:: truth, justice, order and right

ተዋጊ:: teh.wa.gi:: 1) A warrior; One whose very birth proves their fighting spirit. 2)One skilled in fighting ways and/or martial practices. 3) One who studies and practices the Tehwagi Asab. 4) A defender of the "province" ግዛት who strives for success in all endeavours.

ዳንኪራተዋጊ:: da.n.ki.ra teh.wa.gi:: "Warrior Dance" of a specific pattern, a contemporary pan-african rhythm-based cultural (including martial) arts practice involving many dimensions of learning and self-development. This discipline supports mind-breath-body harmony (like yoga, dance or sports can do).

ግዛት:: g.za.t::, The Warrior Province is a region of space (land, air and mind) that the Warrior perceives as their responsibility thus they continually seek to maintain a harmony of peace, power and wisdom throughout their province. In common terms a province (gzat) is a territory governed as a unit of a country or federal republic. Schools of Unified Learning broadens the idea so that it can serve a richer creative, metaphorical and educational purpose, thus a province (gzat) is a region of space (principle aspects; land, air and mind). Land-space (matter) can be viewed as the physical body or the geographic land occupied by persons. Air-space (energy) can be viewed as the air that surrounds and pervades the body (land) or as a aphorism for spirit (relating to breath). Mind-space can be viewed as the domain of consciousness (the mind) or the highest (supreme) and most commonly recognised organising inner principle (intelligence, ንጥር nt'r) in human beings. These ways of coming to know nurture wholesome responsibility and the deepest realisation of key unities revealed through the careful study of the principles of each domain level of the gzat; personal, family, community, nation, earth, universe.

የጥምር ዕውቀት:: yeh.t'.m.r : ur.wu.k'eh.t:: is an Amharic (Ethiopian) term meaning "unified knowledge". unifiedknowledge is an approach to learning (pedagogy) where art, mathematics and the sciences are taught as an integrated one - naturally. It involves dance, visualisation, writing, individual and team work, fun, presentations, logic, challenge, visual arts, reasoning, humour, music creation, multi-media, intuition and creativity in abundance. The practice is nature centred and principle driven. It is comprehensively defined through six objectives and ten principles, processes and protocols (find out more at unifiedknowledge.org).

ብርሃንጨለማ:: b.r.ha.n:ch'eh.leh.ma:: "light without light", a creative term eluding to that which is underlying the electomagnetic spectrum.

የተዋጊ ግዛት:: yeh.teh.wa.gi : g.za.t:: (the symbol) means "Warrior's Province", see province for the basic meaning. This symbol fully sited throughout this guide is a visual icon of the Warrior's Province. Land-space can be viewed as its points and lines. Air-space can be viewed as the areas contained within and outside of the regions of points and lines. Mind-space can be viewed as the principles (laws) of relationship between the points, lines, areas, patterns, perceptions and truths reflective in the domain of consciousness (the mind). This symbol is also used to represent the tehwagi asab. The symbol is a powerful learning resource in unifiedknowledge practice as much information is (and can be) embedded into it.

ትንፋሽ ኣዘዘ:: t.n.fa.sh:ah.zeh.zeh:: breath command practice develop through eleven distinct types of breath command (techniques).

የተዋጊ ኣሳብ:: yeh.teh.wa.gi : a(h).sa.b:: (Warrior's Idea) is expressed as a philosophical utterance (a profound, well reasoned and poetic statement) on the way of the warrior (any person who rises in the face of challenge with the determination to succeed). It is used as a tool of contemplation, sababu (reasoning) and process of agreement. In Schools of Unified Learning all people are viewed as tehwagi (warrior) as their very existenc proves their victory in the initial struggle (challenge) of male and female seeds meeting to form a union (oneness, unity, peace, love).

" The Warrior Idea is the thoughts and perception of the warrior's mind forming clear desires, intentions and plans for the establishment and maintenance of peace throughout their province Through the creation of power and the communication of wisdom, the warrior relentless strives to grasp all of the Tehwagi Asab in the knowledge that the Self of the warrior (i) and the Self of the community (i and i) are One. "

እግዚር ይምስጋን ሐሺማተዋጊ ኣሳብ:: ur.g.z.r:yi.m.s.ga.r ha.shi.ma:teh.wa.gi:a.sa.b:: A greeting and salute expressed at the beginning and conclusion of important events, it means "Creator be praised. Respect the Warrior Idea"

Educating with Unifiedknowledge:
Foundation Course One

Parents and teachers: Is this home learning course for you?

Yes if you wish to become more insightful (and knowledgeable) about the true importance of culture in learning, this can make the difference between your children really connecting to their natural talents and capabilities or them becoming ("maturing" into) self-restricted human beings. Now is the time to look carefully at your own development as an educator. Are you rarely treated to this kind of learning?. Think about it.

High culture; it's more than reading about history, the way people dress or what they eat. Its about total freedom of expression in harmony with One's essential nature and heritage. It's a journey (a process), and **Educating with Unifiedknowledge** will be a step in the right direction that you, your family or learners come to really really value.

How it works:

- Enrol online today
- Instalment payment options available
- Course study pack delivered to your door.
- Follow your study guide, supported by easy to use online learning systems.
- Our tutor teams help you all the way.
- Our learners' cooperative friendly forums provide peer-to-peer support and collective community support.
- Send in your work by post, email, online or bring it into one of our affiliate centres.

Support good causes while you grow.

Your enrolment in this course supports the charitable projects of Abundance Centres (UK) who work globally to strengthen the brilliance of children and their families.

Learn with us:

- Millions of people successfully learn this way.
- A trusted qualification from an organisation with community development integrity and a powerful network of education partners.
- Study from home (and with social networks), at your own pace.
- Full support from your tutors and our administration team.
- Easy to understand course materials

Get more info:
abundancecentre.org/courses
Enrol NOW!

Schools Of Unified Learning

97

Brilliance
@ Abundance Centres (UK)
strengthening the brilliance of the child

- **Making Patterns - Fun-da-Mental Points** (lines, and angles too)

Relating dance movements to fundamental maths ideas gives a stronger internal foundation for young people to build mathematical insight, creativity and enjoyment.

- **Introducing the Art of Mathematics** - Part 1

Mathematics viewed from cultures panAfrica - its simple and omnipresent. Learning the Mathematician's Charter - Keywords explored; observe, record, enjoy, estimate, calculate, forecast, visualise.

- **Reasoning and the Art of Mathematics** - Part 2

Principled visualisation, the greatest purpose of maths. Helping young people value mathematical reasoning, language and empowerment.

- **Number, Measure and Ratio - the old school classics**

These three mathematical ideas have a special depth that when explored can be found to bind many other aspects of maths, the sciences, the arts, nature and general lifeskills studies. There is a great and liberating value when gaining consciousness and competence in them. We explore these old school classics from refreshingly diverse cultural view points.

- **I Count Too - Binary Drumming**

Counting with one hand, counting with two things. Looking at music and number in a deeper way we explore an ancient basis of drum language. Alternate ways of counting combined with rhythmic harmony development make a great way to enhance the value and utility of number.

- **Special Powers in the Hands of Children**

5 important reasonings on power that every child should know, supported by interactive explorations into the meaning of peace development and the realisation of wisdom. Core mathematical ideas as they relate to harmony, energy, work, power and wisdom. Becoming an advance learner.

- **Transformations of Winchi**

Maths taught through dance - the African Crowned Crane bird in rotation, reflection, enlargement and translation. Transformational studies.

> *In this our most popular abunDANCE in Schools workshop we dance like birds (Winchi, the African Crowned Crane), exploring closely how our dance movements and gestures express the mathematical ideas of transformations and other interrelated principles/themes. We work through and practice physical and mental exercises that build determination and mind-breath-body harmonisation. Then, as a grand finale, we bring it all together for the great show, the part of our dance programme we call The Ngoma; bringing principles and free creative expression together naturally in abunDANCE.*

- **ግዛት Gzat: The Province of One**

introducing foundational math principles of space through cultural metaphor. Drawing (visual art) and warrior dance movements combined enhances this multi-sensory learning.

- **Valuing the Quest for Truth**

Ancient views of maths saw a unity of mathematical "truths" with personal and social character development, ethics and justice. Exploring the educative culture of the world's oldest recorded mathematical geniuses and natural philosophers.